GLOBAL GOVERNANCE, TRADE AND THE CRISIS IN EUROPE

GLOBAL GOVERNANCE, TRADE AND THE CRISIS IN EUROPE

MARIAROSARIA IORIO

authorHOUSE®

AuthorHouse™ UK
1663 Liberty Drive
Bloomington, IN 47403 USA
www.authorhouse.co.uk
Phone: 0800.197.4150

Published by AuthorHouse   10/28/2014

ISBN: 978-1-4969-9502-5 (sc)
ISBN: 978-1-4969-9503-2 (e)

Contents

Preface

The end of the Cold War in the late 1980s bolstered people's hope for a better world. The liberal political and economic philosophy presented at the time seemed to provide tools for worldwide economic wealth. Twenty years later, the economic climate is far from what it was expected to be.

Liberal economic thought imploded after the economic and financial crisis beginning in 2008, and now the hopes for a safer and more economically equalized world look remote.

While the economic and financial crisis that began in the United States in 2008 has affected the developed world, the Global South has been indirectly affected by the obsolete governance structures and institutional framework of United Nations (UN) bodies, World Bank and IMF.

The crisis is a starting point for my reflection.

The crisis ravaged the first world's banking system and impacted the Doha Development Round, which was launched by the World Trade Organization (WTO), thereby affecting the chances of developing economies to expand their exports markets and better integrate into the world economy. The Doha Development Agenda (DDA) launched in 2001 seemed, after seven years of negotiations, out of touch with the economic reality and ended up in a standstill.

To date (2014), there is no real sign of any substantial political will to move ahead with a conclusion of the Doha

Round. Actually, this is a dead issue. Negotiations are not on top of the international agenda. The link between the financial crisis and the real economic crisis has, over time, become evident.

This link finally led people to question the whole liberal philosophy that, although fascinating in its political discourse on freedom in all its forms, poses a challenge to economic principles and the role of the State.

The first part of this book contains articles that highlight the main challenges related to global governance structure, trade, and development. They are based on empirical analysis and result from my own professional experiences and observation of international relations and debates. Challenges faced by multilateralism are highlighted.

The second part of this book offers reflections on how the financial crisis has affected Europe, and thoughts on links between educational systems and lack of innovation in Europe.

Europe is stuck in fear and therefore has not managed to mobilize its creative potential to develop innovative solutions for youth and entrepreneurs. Europe looks at what it used to be rather than at what it is to be. European integration should move a step further towards United States of Europe.

Education and training methodologies should be adapted to new economic realities so as to encourage European youth to think creatively and innovatively.

PART I

Global Governance, Trade, and Development

The Global Governance Context Since 2008

The 2008 financial crisis impacted the real economy worldwide. This global crisis has both international and national dimensions.

The international dimension relates, in my view, to the global governance regime.[1] The national dimension relates to national public choices and policies.

Concerning the *global governance regime's* failure to materialize equitable and improved living standards for people worldwide, it is worth recalling that this regime is a result of both *historical* and *political* factors. Since the time of *historic* change marked by the fall of the Berlin Wall in 1989 and the end of the Cold War, *political discourses* on development and economic policies emphasized the role of the private sector, including the financial sector, in development.

As a result of this political shift, these discourses also advocated for cuts in *useless* public expenses, particularly in sectors such as education and health care, and also for

---

[1] A regime is defined as a set of rules and principles that aim to ensure the stability and coherence of the behaviors of different actors on the international scene. A regime is set up to avoid conflicts among states. Explicit or implicit norms, procedures, and regulations for making decisions allow actors' forecasts to converge. See Krasner, S. D., *International Regimes* (New York: Cornell University Press, 1983).

a reduced role of the State in the economy and as a public policy actor. Relying on market forces to achieve economic development was the mantra of economists worldwide. Economic development would have a naturally cascading effect, from the international to the national and local levels. These policy lines proved to be misleading.[2]

Simultaneously, the financial economy has taken center stage in many countries' economies, particularly in industrialized countries. This trend has had catastrophic consequences for both the world economy and worldwide national development policies. Indeed, national authorities decreased oversight of financial sector activities and left the real economy to the market's self-regulatory function. The *market-based*[3] society was indeed supposed to take care of world welfare. Meanwhile, empirical evidence showed that fiscal privileges and privatization of public goods—for

---

[2]   See Iorio, M., *Global Governance, International Development Discourse and National Policy-Making: Highlight of Critical Issues* (Rio de Janeiro: Equit, 2007).

[3]   According to the market-based vision of the world, global wealth would automatically cascade to the vulnerable groups, including women, through the opportunities the market provides. The adoption and implementation of this neoliberal credo limits governments' policy space, both locally and globally. As a result, governments dramatically reduced their roles as guarantors of social justice and as redistributors of economic wealth. The *rights-based approach* to development, which is based on human development as described in the international treaties and declarations and which include equality and equity, accountability, empowerment, and participation, has been taken over by the *market-based approach,* which accounts for the equilibrium between supply and demand of products and services. As a result, the obligations of governments as duty-holders in charge of the protection and promotion of their populations' well-being were voluntarily reduced. At the same time, domestic regulation was mostly thought to be oriented to either protect or open markets. This is the so-called market-based approach.

example, water and electricity—did not automatically result in worldwide economic growth. In many cases, the links between economic growth, production systems and development, and the *virtual economy* were neglected. Policies neglected the polarizing social effects of development policies and market instruments, as well as political dynamics at the local and national level. The current crisis proves that international economic development policies that neglect the political economy of power relations among social groups cannot bring about social justice.

At the national level, *the role of national authorities and their margins of maneuverability* to formulate, implement, and evaluate national economic and financial policies was delegated to the market. At the moment, practically all nations continue to face the challenges posed by the *Washington consensus.*[4]

The reduction of resources available to national authorities to provide services, including essential services, to their populations was part of the public choices and policies of the World Trade Organization (WTO). On the other hand, post-industrial countries gave up the fundamental function of the State as an economic actor to redistribute resources and guarantee social peace and stability. The *real economy* was bypassed by the *virtual economy* of the financial markets. Faith in the market took over even in countries

---

[4]   The Washington consensus includes (i) fiscal discipline, (ii) redirection of public expenditure priorities, (iii) tax reform to broaden the tax base, (iv) interest rate liberalization, (v) a competitive exchange rate and trade liberalization, (vi) liberalization of inflows of foreign direct investment, (vii) privatization, (viii) deregulation to abolish barriers to import and export of products, and (ix) secure property rights.

with a long tradition of social democracy that brought social rights and dialogue into the political sphere. These policy choices resulted in social and political unrest worldwide.

The present architecture of global governance definitely needs to be improved. It must take into account the challenges posed by the services economy as well as the imbalance of international rules, including in trade rules. The existing economic regime's development fundamentals have failed to promote social justice, both nationally and internationally.

At the International Level

(i) *The existing global economic, trade, and financial governance regimes must be rebalanced.* The way to enter into such a process is to hold a large debate among governments' representatives, civil society, and parliaments on rights-based and justice-based international laws. The G20 Summit provided a first step toward a new political framework; however, stakeholders need to discuss this in greater detail. International and national processes have to be based on cooperation rather than competition and also provide a more equitable power balance in the financial and trade-based political economy.

(ii) *The Doha Development Agenda (DDA) must be part of the global rebalancing process and policies.* Trade, indeed, remains a means to complement the development of the real economy. Multilateral trade negotiations must be resumed to consolidate the achievements of the July 2008 package. Instrumentalization of trade rules for national political purposes has damaged developed countries credibility in international relations. Also, a consultative process should be enacted to point out issues regarding which consensuses cannot be achieved in this round; these could eventually become part of the next round of negotiations. Rebalancing the world trading and economic system remains a political choice, one to be made by the major players in world trade. However, it must also be put into the context of the whole set of measures that are to be taken in order to draw the lessons from the current crisis. Leaving the multilateral trading system's rebalancing for "later" would be a mistake. Indeed, the real economy again needs to be put at the center of the rebalancing process, both nationally and globally, and also together with its trade-related issues and policies.[5] As of this writing, the element most in need of being addressed is the need to sustain existing production in the full range of sectors.

(iii) *International (as well as domestic) financial rules must be formulated and implemented to better anticipate actors' behaviors* and to avoid costly emergency situations, the likes of which the system is witnessing nowadays. Public funds used to save private companies do pose a serious problem under the existing rules of governance. The present system has put governments in the uncomfortable position of reacting to the crisis ex post facto, while demonstrating national volatility and instability. The new global regulations should allow action to be taken *ex ante.* To make this possible monitoring and evaluating rules should be put in place.

---

5   For a more detailed analysis of the DDA, see Iorio on the geopolitics of trade negotiations, which is available at: http://www.eldis. org/go/topics/resource-guides/trade-policy/trade-and-gender/ gender-sensitive-trade-policy&id=39161&type=Document.

(iv) *Transparency and accountability* must become the core principles underpinning a new global financial regime.

(v) The idea of *a global financial regulatory body* should continue to be explored. It should not be used to create a bureaucratic superstructure. It should, however, function as a body of surveillance of risk management and transparency in the global banking system (the IMF cannot play such a role). This idea was taken up during the G20. The main question is about the level of responsibility: Should it be at the national or international level? Given the internationalization of the economy, national action is not effective enough. Therefore, an international body should perform the role.

At the National Level

(vi) *The role of the State* should be refocused and strengthened. In particular, the State should be the guarantor of the necessary balance of power in the economic and social spheres.

(vii) *The role of national institutions* needs to be redefined to support market-friendly reforms or to mediate and support redistribution and also ensure social peace.

(viii) The role of markets in societies and of regulation and transparency in risk taking must be changed. The idea of *self-regulated markets and societies* must be replaced by the idea that economic activity should be *embedded*[6]

---

[6] Polanyi, K., "Societies and Economic Systems" in *The Great Transformation: The Political and Economic Origins of Our Time* (Boston:

in social behaviors and aimed at the well-being of entire populations.

(ix) Methods to ensure *clear and open channels of communication* between governments and their populations must be made available to make sure that decision-making at the national level takes into account the interests of the majority, while basing communication on national consultative and negotiating processes.

(x) *Public policies must give priority* to active employment and taxation *to sustain production and services in the real economy.*

(xi) Studies could be performed on how to *shift from an unembedded to a socially embedded* economic paradigm in the realm of services and information technology. Such studies could focus on the role of redistribution policies that aim to ensure sustainable income for people in the services economy.

The Need for Change

The existing global economic and financial governance structure failed to guarantee the necessary stability and predictability of its operations and impacts. It has put millions of people into poverty. Economic activity and global economic growth are not ends in and of themselves. They have to serve human realities and also promote a respect for social and economic rights, including those

---

Beacon Press, 1944), 43.

delivered through economic welfare programs. If economic policies serve a minority against a majority, then they fail in what should be their main mission: building social peace and cohesion. Empirical evidence is confirming that where disparities increase conflicts increase thus negatively affecting economic development. Economic policies have to serve social welfare and ensure well-being for all people. The time has come to put citizens at the center of international and national policy making through national consultation mechanisms and the participation of stakeholders in decision making. Therefore, decisions made by people's representatives are to be in harmony with local needs and aspirations. Social cohesion has to be improved by being worked on over time. Achieving social cohesion demands a constant political dialogue and compromises, as well as political accountability and commitment.

This is not a formula for utopia but, rather, a reminder of the lucidity of those who had realized already in 1944 that *"Poverty anywhere is a threat to prosperity everywhere."*[7]

---

[7] Declaration of Philadelphia, International Labour Office, May 10, 1944.

The Doha Development Agenda (DDA) in the Context of the Global Meltdown: What's Next?

A *Gloomy* Global Economic Context (2009)

The global financial crisis gives rise to questions about an economic system characterized by greed and a lack of transparency. As a result, debates on economic discrimination, evidenced by salary disparities between people who hold top positions and the working class, reemerged.

The real economy is also affected. With it, thousands of workers see their jobs melt away together with the meltdown of the financial economy all over the world. The global economic meltdown understandably influences trade negotiations, particularly the Doha Development Agenda (DDA).

The G20 Mandate: Conclude Modalities in Agriculture and the Non-agricultural Market Access (NAMA) by the End of 2008

After the collapse of the WTO's July 2008 mini-ministerial, people shared a sense that negotiations would remain in a limbo for a while. Then, the financial crisis fully emerged. A G2O[8] meeting took place in Washington on November 15,

---

[8] The G20 on the financial crisis included the participation of Britain, Canada, France, Italy, Japan, Germany, Russia, the United States,

2008, to respond to the financial meltdown and its spread into the real economy. In the declaration resulting from that meeting, the G20 presidents instructed their ministers to reach modalities in agriculture and NAMA by the end of 2008.

Consequently, the chairpersons of the agricultural and NAMA negotiations issued revised modalities texts. Director-General Pascal Lamy of the WTO (since then a new Director General was appointed) was mandated by members to consult with ministers to test their political will in bridging existing gaps, in particular in agriculture, on the *special safeguard mechanism (SSM), and on cotton,* as well as *on the sectorals,* as they apply to the NAMA negotiations. Although these are not the only issues on the DDA, they do remain the issues for which movement is needed in order to go ahead with negotiations in other areas of the DDA.

At this stage of the negotiations, the ministers should politically assess technical advances.

As negotiations proceed by *concentric circles* (from the smaller group to the larger group of members, according to the technical issues up for negotiation), a December 2008

Argentina, Australia, Brazil, China, India, Indonesia, Mexico, Saudi Arabia, South Africa, South Korea, Turkey, and the European Union (under French presidency). Netherlands and Spain were allowed special attendance. The International Monetary Fund, the World Bank, and the Financial Stability Forum were also present. The WTO's G20 on agriculture was attended by Argentina, Bolivia, Brazil, Chile, China, Cuba, Egypt, Guatemala, India, Indonesia, Mexico, Nigeria, Pakistan, Paraguay, Peru, the Philippines, South Africa, Tanzania, Thailand, Uruguay, Venezuela, and Zimbabwe. Information is available at www. wto.org.

mini-ministerial would have been composed of about thirty members, as in July 2008. Had a consensus on the SSM and sectorals been reached among the smaller group of members, then the circle would have been enlarged to negotiate the many other issues that remained on the agenda.

The Landscape of the Negotiations in December 2008

For *the SSM,* divergent political viewpoints on the assessment of the extent of flexibilities needed to use the SSM, in case of import surges. Views continue to differ, as they did in July 2008, on the architecture of the SSM as well as on the links between its duration and domestic prices. This is supposed to be a contingency measure.

The ministers did not tackle the *cotton* issue during the July '08 mini-ministerial, as talks collapsed when they reached the nineteenth issue on the agenda: the SSM. Cotton was the twentieth. There is no modalities text on cotton. This issue was taken up by the director-general of the WTO, who served as the facilitator. He held consultations and arrived at the conclusion that there was both technical and political consensus on this issue. At the technical levels, the reduction in numbers for the items in the Amber and Blue Boxes (trade-distorting subsidies) were apparently discussed. At the press conference held on December 12, 2008, Lamy stated that if the discussions had been only about cotton, he might not have convened the ministers to Geneva.

On sectorals, the main divergence relates to whether or not it would be possible in practice to keep commitments on sectorals (i.e., chemicals and toys, inter alia) nonmandatory.

The major political issue relates to the "*less than full reciprocity*" concept for developing-country members as well as to the fact that sectorals demands came late in the NAMA negotiations. Although transitional implementation time frames were discussed, there was no agreement on whether the ten-year period proposed for implementation for developing countries would be sufficient to guarantee a balanced outcome of the negotiations. Developed members would have five years to implement the plan. This issue reanimates the debate on the greed present within the existing economic system.

No Mini-Ministerial before the End of 2008, and the Way Forward

On the basis of the above-mentioned divergences, ministers were not convened to Geneva to finalize modalities by the end of 2008.

Before the Trade Negotiations Committee (TNC) on December 17, 2008, Pascal Lamy[9] recalled that members had agreed that (i) the DDA mandate should remain unchanged; (ii) regarding agriculture and NAMA, the two texts on the table should be preserved; and (iii) there was more on the DDA than agriculture and NAMA, and that negotiations would benefit from impetus in other areas. He also announced that in *early 2009,* the chairs would continue consultations on NAMA and agriculture. Chairs of the other negotiating groups would also continue their

---

[9]   The full text of Pascal Lamy's speech before the December 17, 2008, Trade Negotiations Committee is available at http://www.wto.org/ english/news_e/news08_e/tnc_dg_stat_17dec08_e.htm.

work; trade facilitation, duty-free, quota-free market access, cotton, and the banana issue would be discussed

The future of the DDA

The mandate of the DDA was clear. As stated by the G33 at the TNC on December 17, 2008, there should be fairness and balance between interests and needs in sectors that were merely commercial nature, and there should be provisions of political comfort for the smallest, most vulnerable, and poorest nations. Furthermore, adding negotiations of new demands based on offensive trade interests endangered the whole idea of the Doha Development Round, while showing that, beyond official statements, there was neither the political commitment nor the will to tackle the development-related items of the DDA.

Aid for Trade[10] and the Doha Development Agenda

To further the Doha Development Round of trade negotiations, the Hong Kong Ministerial Declaration

---

[10] The task force on Aid for Trade was made up of thirteen members: Barbados, Brazil, Canada, China, Colombia, the European Union, Japan, India, Thailand, the United States, and the coordinators of the ACP, African, and LDC groups. The resident representative of Sweden, Ambassador Mia Horn af Rantzien, chaired the task force in a personal capacity. The mandate of the task force was set by paragraph 57 of the Hong Kong Ministerial Declaration, which reads as follows:

> We welcome the discussions of Finance and Development Ministers in various fora, including the Development Committee of the World Bank and IMF, that have taken place this year

instructed the WTO director-general to set up a task force to provide recommendations on how to implement Aid for Trade. In its report to the July 27, 2006, General Council meeting, the task force defined the rationale of Aid for Trade as follows:

> Aid for Trade is about assisting developing countries to increase exports of goods and services, to integrate in the multilateral trading system, and to benefit from the liberalized trade and increased market access. Aid for Trade will enhance growth prospects and reduce poverty in developing countries, as well as complement multilateral trade reforms and distribute the global benefits more equitably across and within countries.

---

on expanding Aid for Trade. Aid for Trade should aim to help developing countries, particularly LDCs, to build the supply-side capacity and trade-related infrastructure that they need to assist them to implement and benefit from WTO Agreements and more broadly to expand their trade. Aid for Trade cannot be a substitute for the development benefits that will result from a successful conclusion to the DDA, particularly on market access. However, it can be a valuable complement to the DDA. We invite the Director-General to create a task force that shall provide recommendations on how to operationalize Aid for Trade. The Task Force will provide recommendations to the General Council by July 2006 on how Aid for Trade might contribute most effectively to the development dimension of the DDA. We also invite the Director-General to consult with Members as well as with the IMF and World Bank, relevant international organisations and the regional development banks with a view to reporting to the General Council on appropriate mechanisms to secure additional financial resources for Aid for Trade, where appropriate through grants and concessional loans.

The task force presented its recommendations at the July 27, 2006, General Council meeting.

However, a Zambian representative on behalf of the LDC group stated the following:

> Aid for Trade has been on-going for long time. More than forty donors, bilateral and multilateral[,] are providing aid in the area of trade for developing countries. What is new is the linkage between aid for trade and the multilateral trade regime, the development emphasis and the Doha Development Agenda (DDA), and recognition by [the] donor community that trade should be actively used as an instrument of development policy to accelerate growth and reduce poverty.[11]

The discourse on the link between the multilateral trade regime negotiations and Aid for Trade puts *trade* at the center of growth-promotion and poverty-reduction strategies at the national, regional, and multilateral levels.

This political and policy shift affects the way development policies and technical cooperation, including gender-related activities, are to be designed and implemented in the future. This will not be done without implications for funding provided for other sectors and aspects of the development policy and implementation.

Mainstreaming of trade in development will also influence technical cooperation assistance requests put forward by developing and LDC WTO members.

---

[11] World Trade Organization, Aid for Trade, WT/AFT/W/22— communication from Zambia on behalf of the LDC group.

This *new* policy orientation raises, nevertheless, a number of critical issues, while animating the debate on the fairness of WTO negotiations and their "developmental" function, as well as the debate on the role of the WTO as a technical cooperation agency (which it is not).

Indeed, the impact of trade negotiations on economic development and social equity remains a "hot" topic, particularly as it concerns aid-related aspects. Many, and oftentimes divergent, opinions and positions are expressed in this regard. These divergent positions reflect different theoretical and political references and rationales. The divergence of views and approaches inspired this article, which intends to be a contribution to the ongoing debate.

Although this aspect of the analysis is not at the core of my argument, it is worth recalling the two main approaches that frame discourses and visions of the role and consequences of trade mainstreaming in development strategies at the global, regional, and national levels. These two perspectives are as follows:

(i) The WTO approach is based on the principles of the liberal and neoliberal economic theory of *comparative advantage and international competitiveness.* According to this perspective, trade liberalization is conducive, although in the long term, to overall economic prosperity and development. For the supporters of this approach, trade is at the core of development policies and constitutes the lens through which economic and social development, including gender equality of treatment have to be perceived and achieved.

(ii)   Social movements and non-governmental organizations (NGOs) are critical of the above-mentioned model. These actors promote a more equitable and solidarity-based world system, thus recognizing the need for international trade rules, albeit different rules than those negotiated in the WTO arena. Indeed, although very promising in theory, the neoliberal vision of the world has not met the expectations of development, as promised by the conclusion of the Uruguay Round. On the contrary, it has increased unemployment, in particular women's worldwide,[12] and widened the gaps between the rich and the poor, resulting in geopolitical instability all over the world.

These two main approaches underpin the rationale and the *philosophical* framework of the analysis of the overall functioning of the world trading system in general. They also specify the means to be put in place to achieve economic development. In addition, they raise a number of questions that concern both the general principles and the specifics of the *development and Aid for Trade trend,* in both the WTO and other development agencies.

Aid for Trade is to be situated in the context of provisions for special and differential treatment for LDCs, as defined by the WTO agreements, including implementation periods (recalled in Annex 1 of the agreement); ministerial decisions

---

[12]   Liberalization accompanied by the disengagement of the State in the context of structural adjustment programs (SAPs) in most developing countries has resulted in a decrease in the number of women holding positions in socially valued employment sectors, in increased occupational segregation, and in a lack of access to appropriate training. Women remain mostly employed in temporary, part-time, casual, and home-based work.

and declarations in favor of LDCs (Annex 2); and WTO provisions for developing countries (Annex 3).

Aid for Trade is (and shall remain) a subitem of aid for development, as pointed out by Zambia in its communication on behalf of the LDC group (WT/AFT/W/22). It should not become a substitute for other development and international cooperation activities.

Aid for Trade might be eventually implemented without the conclusion of the Doha Development Round. It should not expand the WTO's field of action with regard to technical cooperation and training programs.[13] Activities that do not fall within the WTO mandate should be picked up by other organizations.

The task force on Aid for Trade has identified the following *main sectors of activities* that are in Aid for Trade's scope:

(i)   trade policy and regulations, including training, analysis, and capacity building, to comply with WTO rules and standards;

(ii)   trade development, including market analysis and development;

(iii) building supply-side capacity and trade-related infrastructure to facilitate market access and greater exports;

---

[13] Aid for Trade's implementation should not be linked to the negotiations taking place in the context of the Doha Development Agenda. It should be implemented independently from the results of the Doha Round.

(iv)   building productive capacity;

(v)   trade-related adjustment, including putting in place measures to benefit from trade liberalization;

(vi)   assisting regional and global integration;

(vii) assisting the implementation of WTO agreements.

The guiding principles of Aid for Trade will be those enounced in the Paris Declaration on Aid Effectiveness, namely country ownership, alignment of Aid for Trade to the national development goals for 2010; donors' coordination; harmonization of donors' procedures; and program-based aid modalities, transparency, and multiyear commitments. *Aid for Trade should be rendered in a coherent manner, taking full account of, among other things, the gender perspective and the overall goal of sustainable development.*

(A) The Theoretical References

In the task force's recommendations, *mainstreaming of trade* in developmental policy appears to be *the means* to promote growth, development, and poverty reduction and to achieve the Millennium Development Goals (MDG).

The macroeconomic theory of supply and demand[14] inspired the task force's document and is applied to the formulation and implementation of Aid for Trade.

---

[14]   *Supply* is the quantity that producers are willing to sell at a given price. The main determinants of supply are the market price of goodsand their production costs. In fact, supply curves are constructed from the industries long-run production costs, including labour costs. *Demand* is

This theoretical reference does not come without consequences, as it is the milestone of the world trading system. Although, supporters of the existing liberal trading system proclaim that international trade has achieved its results in terms of global economic growth, empirical evidence shows that it still has not succeeded in lifting citizens out of poverty. Indeed, it jeopardizes employment and incomes at the regional and national level.

In this regard, at least three main questions can be asked when examining the implementation of Aid for Trade as it was planned:

(i)   How will Aid for Trade impact export-related infrastructure?

(ii) What will be the impact of Aid for Trade on local and national social preferences and production systems?

(iii) How are donors planning to face this shift of preferences and the loss of jobs deriving from adjustment costs of trade liberalization in developing countries?

The risk is that, while Aid for Trade raises expectations, it might still leave weaker trading partners in a dependent position vis-à-vis international markets. Main structural production-system imbalances will persist, and redistribution policy issues might remain unsolved, as national authorities face the consequences of adjustment costs.

---

the quantity of a good that consumers are not only willing to purchase but also have the capacity to buy at the given price per unit at the time.

(B) Adjustment Costs

The recommendations also state that Aid for Trade should address the supply and infrastructural constraints of developing and LDC WTO members and also help these countries to better (i) adjust to trade liberalization; (ii) integrate regionally and internationally; and (iii) implement WTO agreements.

These objectives are too ambitious when compared to the available resources.

As generally acknowledged, adjustment costs in most countries result mostly from preference erosion, loss of tariff revenue, loss of employment, adjustment to the expiration of the Agreement on Textiles and Clothing, high food prices, weak supply-side responses, social costs from job losses and retraining, increases in interest rates, and cross-country effects of tariff cuts.

In this respect, in 2003, the IMF estimated that a 40 per cent cut in the most-favored nation (MFN) tariffs of Quad countries (the United States, Japan, Canada, and the European Union) would result in a potential aggregate value of export revenue loss for LDCs of about $530 million per year. For middle-income developing countries, the loss was about $914 million for middle-income developing countries

In this context, Aid for Trade could not be the development solution to adjustment costs, including diversification into new products, finding alternative sources of fiscal revenue, retraining and retooling employees to facilitate social adjustment, and helping enterprises adapt to a more competitive trading environment.[15]

This is not only a practical but also a political issue. A number of points should be mentioned in this regard.

On the one hand, developed countries' trade policies impede poorer countries from accessing rich markets for their goods, while also distorting international trade. International aid should not be used to compensate for a lack of market access. Furthermore, for developing countries, which are currently unable to take advantage of existing market access possibilities in developed countries, funds provided under Aid for Trade will not be enough to address supply-side constraints.

Developing countries, which have had to adjust to losing a niche in developed countries' markets as a result of the phasing out of the Agreement on Textiles and Clothing and the new sugar market conditions, will not be able to succeed in the current system of economies of scale.

The contradiction remains evident as both bilateral and multilateral donors are ready to enter into Aid for Trade to increase developing countries' and the LDCs' participation in the world trading system.

---

[15] This comes from the report on a conference organized by the United Nations Conference for Trade and Development (UNCTAD) and the Commonwealth Secretariat, United Nations, New York and Geneva, 2006.

(C) Trade Mainstreaming and Development

The task force clearly states that *mainstreaming trade into national development strategies is the key to the effectiveness of Aid for Trade.* As a result, actions that should be taken at the national, regional, and global levels are identified. The task force also emphasizes the link between economic growth and trade liberalization as a means to stimulate growth and reduce poverty.

This emphasis feeds into the main negotiating positions of developing and LDC WTO members who articulate their needs in terms of increased access to Global Northern developed countries' markets.owever, on this point, a number of questions arise:

(i) Is increased market access the solution to development-related issues?

(ii) Will this perspective be replaced by a larger policy space and autonomy at the national level, including a gender-sensitive production system that creates equitable employment opportunities?

(iii) Should national autonomy and institutional development aim to face national economic redistribution of wealth and gender-equitable social policies?

These questions present a different scenario from the one based on market access. Also, they stress the national policy autonomy dimension while raising issues of political philosophy, i.e., production systems, social democracy, redistribution of trade revenues, and autonomous alternative policy making (as opposed to autonomous trade liberalization). Indeed, a number of studies have demonstrated that growth and trade are not enough to reduce poverty. To do that requires national redistribution and social policies put in place by national governments to guarantee citizens' control and choices. Trade policies can neither replace economic policies nor be used as development tools. They remain part of a global development plan and are only a part of the "development story telling". The idea of using trade a development tool is proving weak in reality.

(D) Country Eligibility, Monitoring, and Evaluation

As Envisaged by the Task Force

In principle, all developing countries and LDCs will be eligible for Aid for Trade, as noted in the Hong Kong Ministerial Declaration. However, given the WTO's self-eligibility procedure, the eligibility criteria for Aid for Trade should be further clarified, along with indicators of success or failure. This is part of the monitoring and evaluation phase.

In recipient countries, Aid for Trade is to be monitored with regard to aid mainstreaming, identification of priority needs, donor responses, and progress made in implementing trade-related projects and programs as well as the impact of these efforts. Evaluation of in-country processes should focus on, among other things, the progress of mainstreaming trade in national development plans. Evaluations should adopt a results-based approach in order to ensure the effectiveness of Aid for Trade programs in relation to their objectives.

As far as donors are concerned, they *should report on the content of such commitments as well as on how they plan to meet the targets for Aid for Trade that the donors have announced.*[16]

As I See It

Monitoring and evaluation are to be provided with clear objectives and program formulation and implementation. My experience with UN executing agencies has shown that stating general principles is not enough to guarantee the effective use of aid.

Past experience has shown that monitoring and evaluation should take into account not only institutional mechanisms, but also underpinning principles as well as the outcomes of assistance programs.

Quantifiable criteria of evaluation (this is an indicative list to be accompanied by qualitative assessment) should include whether or not Aid for Trade has done the following:

(i)   lifted nationals out of poverty by raising their incomes in a stable and sustainable manner;

(ii)   increased beneficiaries' production and exports, of which a percentage is the result of Aid for Trade;

(iii)   ensured that building infrastructure has benefited the whole population, in particular women as the main care-economy actors;

---

[16] WT/AFT/1.

(iv)   seen that trade has been beneficial to local producers and local distribution chains;

(v)   reoriented monocrop export-led agricultural production to self-reliant and diversified production aimed at solving malnutrition and famines;

(vi)   resulted (wherever possible) in national industrialization plans;

(vii) promoted services that are of interest to the overall well-being of local populations.

On the basis of the above, the following points are to be stressed:

Role of Trade in National Development Policy Making

Without denying its contribution to world welfare, we should continue to perceive trade as a sub-item of development, not *the means*—and certainly not *the only means* to achieving or maintaining economic growth and development;

Trade needs should be put in the larger context of national social and political strategies and preferences not to be the condition sine qua non for shaping national socially equitable development policies.

The Role of Aid for Trade in National Policy Making

Aid for Trade should not become a sub-item of World Bank programs, which remain a revamped version of structural adjustment programs (SAPs), but should be a sub-item of national autonomous policy making centered on social-friendly economic policies.

Aid for Trade should go beyond general policy declarations related to *gender-sensitive policy and sustainable development.*[17] It should be part of a specific global plan for sectors aimed at improving female employment and working conditions wherever possible, e.g., higher employment standards and more stable and sustainable income.

Aid for Trade should indeed be monitored and evaluated. This process should take place in light of clearly stated objectives and both qualitative and quantitative criteria. Formulating appropriate national regulatory frameworks should be a priority activity, in particular for LDCs and lower-income developing countries.

Aid for Trade should address main production system imbalances, in particular to reduce external dependency and support transformation of monoculture productions into a more self-sustained and development-friendly production system at the national, regional, and global levels.

In conclusion, independent of whether or not Aid for Trade will be linked to the continuation of the DDA negotiations, the reflection on the evolution of Aid for Trade in context of both the WTO and other agencies raises a number of issues that relate, on one hand, to the rationale underpinning Aid for Trade.

---

[17] World Trade Organization, W/AFT/1.

On the other hand, evaluation remains central. Indicators of success (or failure) taking into account both quantitative and qualitative aspects of development should be set to ensure the appropriate and truly sustainable implementation of Aid for Trade.

Such an approach would avoid undermining ongoing national development efforts and resulting in even more disrupted local social and production realities. Nevertheless, when analyzing the contemporary international production system through the lens of social reciprocity and redistribution as well as gender social symmetry, citizens of the world can easily assess how harmful the impact of the existing production and trading system can be on national social and political stability.

Aid for Trade will not be enough to face these challenges. It is definitely not the *policy link* necessary to lift people out of poverty and guarantee sustainable gender-sensitive development in the world.

From the Task Force Recommendations (2006) to the Second Global Review

(July 6–7, 2009)

Aid for Trade was launched in 2006 at a time when the financial crisis was not yet on the horizon, and the Doha Development Agenda (DDA) seemed to be on track to conclude (not without difficulties). Three years after the task force (TF) recommendations on Aid for Trade (2006), the second global review on Aid Trade was undertaken with high expectations, despite the gloomy context in which it took place.

Indeed, the deadlock of the DDA negotiations as of July 2008 and the financial crisis give this second global review of Aid for Trade a rather important symbolic value.

Furthering the Doha Development Round of trade negotiations, the Hong Kong Ministerial Declaration instructed the WTO director-general to set up a task force to provide recommendations for how to implement Aid for Trade.

In its report to the July 27, 2006, General Council meeting, the task force defined the rationale of Aid for Trade as follows:

> Aid for Trade is about assisting developing countries to increase exports of goods and services, to integrate in the multilateral trading system, and to benefit from the liberalized trade and increased market access. Aid for Trade will enhance growth prospects and reduce poverty in developing countries, as well as complement multilateral trade reforms and distribute the global benefits more equitably across and within countries.

The task force on Aid for Trade identified the scope of Aid for Trade: (i) instituting trade policy and regulations, including training, analysis, and capacity building, to comply with WTO rules and standards; (ii) developing trade, including market analysis and development; (iii) building the supply-side capacity and trade-related infrastructure to facilitate market access and increased exports; (iv) building productive capacity; (v) making trade-related adjustments, including putting in place measures for countries to benefit from trade liberalization; (vi) assisting regional and global integration; and (vii) assisting in implementing WTO agreements.

The recommendations also stated that Aid for Trade should address the supply and infrastructural constraints of developing and LDC WTO members and help these countries to better (i) adjust to trade liberalization; (ii) integrate regionally and internationally; and (iii) implement WTO agreements.

The general theoretical assumptions of mainstreaming trade in development as well as the methodological aspects of monitoring and evaluating Aid for Trade were analyzed in the 2006 paper: "Aid for Trade and the Doha Development Agenda (DDA): Finding the Policy Link." The article aimed to provide a contribution on the occasion of the second global review (July 6–7, 2009) of the challenges ahead, including regional integration and Aid for Trade as well as Aid for Trade's physical infrastructure.

Regional Integration and Aid for Trade

Aid for Trade does not operate in a vacuum. It is worth recalling the salient systemic trends observed since it was launched in 2006. First, regionalism has accelerated over the past few years, so Aid for Trade is presented as a new opportunity for economic development and for preparing developing countries to come out of the crisis. The increasing number of regional agreements poses a systemic challenge to the multilateral trading system, particularly as multilateral negotiations continue to be deadlocked.

Initiatives were taken to tackle these challenges. The 2006 decision to fast-track the transparency mechanism negotiated in the Doha Round resulted from the need to better understand what was going on in many different regional trade agreements (RTAs).

Speaking to the same dynamic, Pascal Lamy stated in his speech of April 29, 2009, to the General Council, "We should collectively think about some way of gradually "multilateralizing" concessions made in free trade agreements.

Indeed, the relationship between multilateral and regional dynamics raises a number of questions about Aid for Trade. These are as follows: How will the regional integration processes, including South–South initiatives, affect Aid for Trade's allocation of resources? Should regional allocation of resources take over the national allocation of Aid for Trade funds to make sure that sectors of regional interest, such as infrastructure, are handled by regional coordination units? How should regional and national entities divide responsibility in the implementation process?

(i) Should Aid for Trade be part the monitoring mechanism of RTAs it is already part of the trade policy reviews)?

Should Aid for Trade also include technical assistance related to the eventual harmonization of trade rules and regulations whenever needed in the articulation between regional and multilateral agreements?

These questions are to be answered in the implementation phase, as they relate to the streamlining of resources allocation and can affect the impact of Aid for Trade.

Infrastructure and Aid for Trade

The importance of physical infrastructure is now generally acknowledged as one of the fundamentals (following the strengthening of productive capacity) to increase trade, both regionally and globally. This section will highlight a few selected questions/issues.

They are as follows:

(i) African countries identified the rehabilitation of railways (which are easier to maintain than roads in the long term) and the improvement of energy distribution networks (electricity cuts affect production) as priorities for their supply-side capacity building. These two sectors are noted as strategic in development policies. In light of its strategic and geopolitical implications, can Aid for Trade effectively and sustainably tackle energy-related constraints, including distribution-related aspects?

(ii) The North–South Corridor seems to be a first step; however, the long-term aspects of this approach remain to be developed. Is this corridor a sustainable project?

(iii) Connecting national developing economies with global and regional economies is high on the agenda of the Aid for Trade discussions. Are donors ready to tackle the challenges of connectivity on the internal level, between rural and urban areas within countries? In many developing regions, rural areas remain cut off from the urban centers. Small farming production units, which are usually managed by women, have no access to the export markets or to the marketing channels at the national level.

(iv) Efforts must continue if Aid for Trade is to address specific constraints of small-scale exporters in meeting international technical standards, particularly with regard to test procedures, information technology (energy distribution is strictly related to this aspect of the debate), packaging, and risk management, to name only a few.

Consultation of Stakeholders

It is now more and more common to hear that the private sector is to be consulted and be part of the implementation of Aid for Trade. That makes sense from the perspective of the stakeholders, who ensure that the priorities identified match their needs. A note of caution shall, however, be expressed.

The discourse of trade and trade policy is already the domain of the private sector, as, by definition, trade flows are mostly piloted by the private sector. Governments must, however, ensure that any self-assessment of needs processes takes into account the whole range of needs, not only those of the more structured and visible private-sector actors.

The emerging private-sector actors, namely the small number of self-employed women in the informal and services sectors, are also to be included in the consultation process. In many cases, these sectors employ over 70 percent of the local population and have great export potential that does not materialize.

Do Few Things Well

Development needs are enormous. Resources remain inadequate to meet the challenges ahead. Nevertheless, Aid for Trade has been a useful tool for beginning to tackle some of the major constraints related to trade facilitation in developing and least developed countries. It has been a step toward a long-term goal: rebalancing an unbalanced economic global system.

According to this perspective, its implementation had to be focused, streamlined, and guided by accountability and transparency.

The WTO, as a global monitoring body of trade policy, must set a clear and objective-oriented methodology for monitoring and evaluating Aid for Trade activities (the self-assessment methodology raises doubts about the objective assessment of Aid for Trade's impact and effectiveness). Efforts must be made to keep Aid for Trade realistic and functional, as it was framed by the task force in 2006 (there is a tendency to divert from the TF recommendations).

Governments have to make sure that knowledge and information are widespread to national stakeholders, including small farmers, women groups, and informal-sector actors who are not in the official private-sector category.

Hopes Not to Be Deceived

The following was stated by a Zambian representative on behalf of the LDC group:

> Aid for Trade has been on-going for a long time. More than forty donors, bilateral and multilateral [,] are providing aid in the area of trade for developing countries. What is new is the linkage between Aid for Trade and the multilateral trade regime, the development emphasis and the Doha Development Agenda (DDA), and recognition by [the] donor community that trade should be actively used as an instrument of development policy to accelerate growth and reduce poverty.

This statement becomes more important in the present global economic and political crisis, particularly in the context of the real economy, where jobs are created and where growth potential, if accompanied by appropriate public policies, can lift people out of poverty.

For those (fewer and fewer) who continue to believe in the multilateral trading system, Aid for Trade is a complement to the efforts that have to be made to rebalance trade rules so as to provide real economic opportunities to industrial and agricultural goods producers and service providers from developing and emerging economies. Hopes cannot be deceived.

The credibility of multilateralism has been weakened by lack of concrete results beyond slogans and political declarations. In fact, a few years later hopes have been deceived and peace has not been achieved through trade. Inequalities persist. Poor become poorer and rich become richer. What's wrong?

Health Services: Public or Tradable Services?

Corporations and multinationals, who are the winners in the neo-liberal system, succeeded in propagating the idea that the market needs little or no regulation, as it can regulate itself through the *invisible hand*.

According to this vision of the world, global wealth would automatically cascade to the vulnerable groups, including women, through the opportunities provided by the market.

The adoption and implementation of this neoliberal credo limited governments' policy space, both locally and globally. As a result, governments dramatically reduced their roles as guarantors of social justice and as redistributors of economic wealth, including through public health-care provisions.

As a result, positive obligations of governments as duty-holders in charge of the protection and promotion of their populations' well-being were voluntarily reduced. At the same time, domestic regulation was thought to be mostly oriented toward either protecting or opening markets. The market-based approach and the subsequent withdrawal of states from rights-based domestic regulation further shrank the chances for health care for all people worldwide.

Once again, the market became the regulator of both economic and social development, globally and locally. These political choices weakened the capacity of national authorities to take appropriate regulatory actions to guarantee access to health care for all. The neoliberal paradigm contributed, therefore, to the increase in invisible barriers for the most vulnerable groups to accessing health-care (as well as education and electricity) services worldwide.

Gaps in opportunities between men and women and between a wealthy minority and a poor majority increased over time. As the market role in the political and social policy discourses increased, the scope of action to guarantee access to health-based services decreased.

By opening essential services to private investors, national policy makers created two-speed health-care systems, one for the wealthy minority and one for the poor majority.

Furthermore, the lack of protection for national strategic and essential sectors resulting from structural adjustment programs and states' disengagement from public-services management set a negative trend in the effort to provide health care for all.

A clear separation should be kept between commercial and social services sectors, including health care. The main objective of national regulatory frameworks should be egalitarian development policies and distribution of wealth to ensure all people's access to health-care services. Economic and trade regulatory frameworks are to ensure a balance of power between the different economic actors. Such frameworks should be based on the principle of social justice.

To achieve these goals, it is a prerequisite to strengthen State capacity to formulate and implement progressive development and social policies, without which the commercial interests

Mariarosaria Iorio

of a few will prevail over economic justice and equitable redistribution of wealth for the majority of people.

The market-based approach, which is based on the equilibrium between the supply and demand of products and services, cannot be applied to public health-care services. Health care should not be a tradable service. Health should not be marketable but, rather, should be considered as a common good of societies. In light of this, health-care services must be provided free of charge.

A rights-based domestic regulation rather than market-based regulation is therefore fundamental to guarantee free access to health-care services for all. It is also a tool to effectively respond to the needs of vulnerable groups, which face economic shocks.

The current global economic system is, no doubt, full of contradictions and inconsistencies that resulted from the focus on short-term rather than long-term policies, as well as from the wrong assumption that global wealth and economic development would automatically benefit all. In fact, without redistribution policies and accountability of public action wealth is captured only by a minority. Such a situation does endanger social stability by limiting access of vulnerable groups, in particular women and youth to income generating activities.

The market-based approach has proven to be contradictory to a rights-based approach of policy-making at the national level. A rights-based approach would put development of the human majority at its heart. Putting humankind's well-being at the center of development is necessary if we are to concretely work towards more egalitarian and equitable societies, nationally and internationally. Access to health care for all is a prerequisite for worldwide development.

The economic crisis is not a justification to dismantle social safety nets both in developing and industrialized countries. On the contrary, a minimum of social protection is necessary to maintain social peace.

A Changing Global Agenda: Climate Change and Trade

What About Development?

Too many times, globalization has wrongly allowed multinationals to disregard both environmental and labor standards. Existing unsustainable production and consumption systems resulted, over time, in increased energy use and decreased energy supplies, as well as in increased emissions of gas carbon, which has contributed to climate change. This is an issue that will mark the forthcoming global agenda.

In the context of preparing for the international Climate Change Conference in Denmark in 2009 (and in more recent meetings, i.e. in New York), a number of development-related issues were highlighted. The most recurrent related to the following:

(i)   the intersection between climate change and sustainable development policies, including food security and sustainable agriculture;

(ii)   the costs of clean technology transfer and its impact on production and exports;

(iii) issues related to intellectual property rights;

(iv)   commitments to reduce carbon gas emissions and energy prices;

(v) special and differential treatment to respond to differentiated levels of responsibilities with regard to pollution in industrialized and developing countries.

What Is the Intersection between Trade Rules and Climate Policy?

Persisting imbalances in existing production and consumption models as well as in existing international trade rules intersect with the development aspects of the climate change debates.

The climate change negotiations will inevitably highlight existing contradictions within the multilateral trading system with regard to its sustainable development objective, as was announced in the preamble of the Marrakech Agreement establishing the WTO and its existing rules. Some intersections include the following main principles and rules:

(i) Processes and production methods (PPMs) and the non-discrimination principle. WTO members cannot discriminate against a product on the basis of its production history (e.g., the shrimp case);

(ii) Subsidies in agriculture, as they encourage overproduction, in particular in the industrialized agriculture sector;

(iii) Trade-related intellectual property rights (TRIPS) and the transfer of clean technologies and knowhow. As intellectual property rights are not owned by governments but, rather, by private companies, the issue here is how developing countries can benefit from technology transfer. In Bali, the possibility of using the same approach that is used for TRIPS and medicines was discussed vis-à-vis clean technology transfer. No agreement was reached on this issue.

(iv) Inappropriate use of tax border measures, which might be put in place by industrialized countries to compensate for the costs of cleaner technology. This could become a hidden barrier to the trade of products originating from developing countries and that are produced by multinationals which have their headquarters in the industrialized world. A global fund under the Millennium Development Goals (MDG)s to finance clean technology transfer was proposed in Bali.

Voices from the Global South have already stressed that negotiations on climate change should not become an excuse to further limit developing countries' chances to achieve economic and social development by shifting the burden onto those countries. Therefore, in dealing with carbon emission targets and energy pricing, the issues of transparency and development objectives must be taken into account.

India, Australia, and Indonesia have national plans to reach their own carbon-emission targets. Trade negotiations in the framework of the Doha Development Agenda are deadlocked. One issue on the table was tariff quota creation. This issue has implications for identifying sensitive products and smaller tariff reductions. The payment for the smaller tariff reduction is a tariff quota.

If states are not allowed to create new quotas, then only products that currently have quotas could be sensitive.

The New Geopolitics of Trade and the Collapse of the Mini-Ministerial (July 2008) of the WTO: Was It *Only* about the Special Safeguard Mechanism?

The Geopolitical Context

The collapse of negotiations during the WTO mini-ministerial (July 21–31, 2008) reflected the new geopolitics of the world economy. The emerging economies with large proportions of their populations employed in agriculture were at the heart of the negotiating processes and were put at the forefront of finding another way to approach trade issues. This way puts people's livelihoods at the center of decision-making in international trade negotiations.

Two main visions of the world emerged from the talks. One of these was based on market access as a means to ensure economic growth and promote economic development. The other vision was based on protecting farmers' livelihoods. These two lines of political thought were there all along during the negotiating process, and were reflected in the technical aspects of the negotiations. This is not new. What is new is that more and more actors in the negotiations are convinced that some issues can no longer be left to market regulation. Poverty and people's livelihoods demand specific actions and strong positions.

Issues at Stake

One can understand the surprise of those who say that the collapse was not *"only"* about the SSM[1]. It would, however, be misguided to think that this issue was too "small" to made the talks collapse. In countries where 60 percent of the population is composed of small farmers (mostly women) and where imports surges could displace millions of people, the SSM acquires major political value.

There were twenty issues on the agenda of the mini-ministerial. The special safeguard mechanism (SSM) was nineteenth on the agenda. The G33, represented in the G7 by India, announced from the beginning that the SSM was linked to livelihood and therefore was not negotiable. More than a hundred other developing countries supported this position. The G20 (which was more concerned with diversified economies and interests) had discussed the issue of the SSM but found no common position.

Was the SSM the *"only"* reason for the collapse? Given the architecture of the "package" and the sequencing of issues, the SSM was to be followed by cotton subsidies. The Hong Kong Ministerial Declaration says, that: "We recall the mandate given by the Members in the Decision adopted by the General Council on 1 August 2004 to address cotton ambitiously, expeditiously and specifically, within the agriculture negotiations in relation to all trade-distorting policies affecting the sector." This issue was not discussed.

The cotton issue was of particular interest to the Western African countries (Benin, Burkina Faso, Chad, and Mali) whose producers suffer because of competition from rich countries, which subsidize cotton.

Then, looking back at other specific issues on the table in agriculture, the approach of exchanging overall trade-distorting subsidies (OTDS) in agriculture for market access in emerging agricultural markets and for nonagricultural market access again reflected a political choice that linked growth to market access and to the so-called offensive interests. This argument was not convincing to those who have defended all along the need to protect the weakest segments of their societies, i.e., small farmers (who are mostly women) and petty traders.

The principles of *less-than-full reciprocity* and *special and differential treatment* for developing countries as referred to in the Doha Declaration were lost in the process. A Swiss formula coefficient of 8 for the United States and the European Union represented, as stated by Argentina, a cut slightly over 42 percent, while a coefficient of 20 for some countries, including flexibilities, would have meant a cut of 60 percent. This would have also meant a cut two-thirds lower for developed countries than for developing countries. "It is less than full reciprocity inversely applied for the benefit of the main trading partners," a representative for Argentina said. This action would have been against less-than-full reciprocity and paragraph 24 of the Hong Kong Ministerial Declaration. The NAMA numbers were asked to be changed, and the conditions that were attached (sectorals in exchange for more flexibilities and better coefficients) were asked to be eliminated.

The lesson from this collapse is that there is a political economy of global trade just as there is the political economy of national policy making. The perception of what is important and what is minor in international negotiations is linked to the constituencies of those who negotiate as well as to a new geopolitics of trade policy. The context of the Uruguay Round has changed as well as the context of the launching of the Doha Round. As some developing countries are now emerging economies and have a voice in the world trading system, the financial crisis has affected industrialized countries. This new context has diverted attention from trade issues.

Is There Anything New with the Post-2015 United Nations (UN) Agenda on Sustainable[18] Development?

What Are the Issues?

As the world undergoes a major systemic crisis, commitment to redistribution, social well-being, and environmental justice is central. However, there is also a need to concretely and positively impact populations across the world at all levels of the social scale.

In light of the above, the post-2015 UN agenda faces a number of weaknesses:

* First, the assessment of the Millennium Development Goals' (MDGs) impact is not over yet. As a result, there is no basis to build upon. No one knows what worked and what did not work with the MDG. The MDG objectives were evidently not achieved, as the debates on

---

[18] Sustainable development "posits a desirable future state for human societies in which living conditions and resource-use meet human needs without undermining the sustainability of natural systems and the environment, so that future generations may also have their needs met. Sustainable development ties together concern for the carrying capacity of natural systems with the social and economic challenges faced by humanity. This concept has been used for the first time by the Brundtland Report: *Our Common Future*[,] published by the United Nations['] World Commission on Environment and Development (WCED) in 1987.

poverty alleviation continue and as development actors seem to look for new tools.

- Second, policy issues related to poverty alleviation are of national concern. It appears very difficult to deal with these issues at the international level. Poverty-related issues must be a part of national commitment and of governments' strategic plans, which the United Nations cannot take care of.

- Third, the methodology for fixing the post-2015 agenda is not clear. Attainment of the sustainable development goals (SDGs) might not happen either. In fact, inserting environmental and social policies into the poverty-alleviation debates is not new. Where do these interests come from? How were they put on the UN agenda? The answer seems clear: These are not development issues, but rather postdevelopment policy issues. No country has been able to achieve economic development without polluting and without the sacrifices made by people of many generations. I am thinking about the industrialization in Europe.

Its targets were multilateralism and interdependence of nations in the search for a sustainable development path. The report sought to recapture the spirit of the United Nations Conference on the Human Environment—the Stockholm Conference—which had introduced environmental concerns to the formal political development sphere. *Our Common Future* placed environmental issues firmly on the political agenda; it aimed to discuss the environment and development as one single issue. The document was the culmination of a '900 day' international exercise which catalogued, analyzed, and synthesized written submissions and expert testimony from 'senior government representatives, scientists and experts, research institutes, industrialists, representatives of nongovernmental organizations, and the general public' held at public hearings throughout the world" ("Our Common Future," *Wikipedia* [last updated September 30, 2014], http://en.wikipedia.org/wiki/Our_Common_Future).

- Four, if funds for the MDG are not available, then what will happen with the SDGs? Why would governments invest more than in the past in a period of profound economic crisis?

Furthermore, there are the technical dimensions of the relationship between economic development and environmental and social policies to consider. The assumption is that economic development is characterized by different stages of economic activity and that there is a progressive approach to be taken when formulating environmental and social policies.

What Are the Positions?

In this regard, positions diverge. They can be summarized as follows:

(a) On the one hand, environmentalists, particularly in industrialized countries, say that sustainable development, in general and its environmental dimension, in particular is compatible with economic competitiveness and growth, even at early stages of economic development. Therefore, environmental policies are not only compatible but also necessary for economic development if it is to benefit all generations. For supporters of the environment as a common good of humanity, sustainable development must be a priority on the development agenda, in spite of its economic costs. On the other hand, there are those who affirm that environmental protection is an unaffordable production cost, particularly at early stages of development. Environment would even be a "trade hidden barrier"[19] created by industrialized countries to impede the faster access of emerging countries' products to richer markets, thereby impeding the economic development of infant industries in developing and emerging economies;

(b)   Regarding the elitist *market-based approach* applied to essential services, namely health care and education, rights-based activists highlight that basic services should be accessible to all, and in particular to the poor. Naturally, a market-based approach would result in private provision of services and more expensive services, which would be not accessible to the poorest segments of society.

My Position on Environment-Friendly Production Systems

As the global economy functions on the principles of the *comparative advantage* theory, countries all over the world have generally adopted the idea that countries grow according to what they specialize in and *can do better* than other countries when it comes to trading in goods and/or services.

In practice, such an assumption means that trading in products and services facilitates consumers' access to cheaper products, both at the national and international level.

In this view, methods and processes of production are central. Industrial production at early stages of development

---

[19]   Ségolène Royal (current French minister of ecology) stated that ecology should not be "punitive."

is a polluting activity unless environmental technology is adopted at the early stages of industrialization. This implies extra costs that will negatively impact the prices of products, making them more expensive on the global market and, therefore, less competitive.

Many industries refuse, therefore, to use environmental technology, as they consider it to be an obstacle to their competitiveness in the global market. This position has been often put on the table by the governments of emerging economies and developing countries, especially when it comes down to, for example, linking trade rules and the environment.

How to make environmental investments affordable? Is environment a "concern for rich people only"? These questions remain open as the debates continue. In fact, a number of elements must be addressed.

If we assume that, beyond some turning point, the use of the natural resources and/or the emission of wastes declines as income increases, as stated by Kuznets in 1955,[20] then we could also say that the environmental issues have to be read through the lens of (i) types of production and consumption; (ii) reasons for the preference for environment quality; (iii) institutions that are needed to internalize externalities; and (iv) increasing returns to account for costs associated with pollution abatement.

In sum, environmental issues have to be read through the lens of stages of economic development. Unless environmental technologies become affordable and accessible, it appears

---

[20] Kuznets S., "Economic Growth and Income Inequality," *The American Economic Review* 45, no. 1 (March 1955): 1–18.

that, at early stages of industrial production, polluting practices are inevitable.

Access to technology is a key factor. Now, access to technology has a strategic aspect. Interests in this sector are diverging, of course, between those who produce technology and those who need to use it but do not have the production capacity to innovate, namely developing countries.

Open Questions on the Environment and SDGs

Are the SDGs going to take into account these factors? And how is the international community to face these challenges? Is a progressive time schedule foreseen?

My Position on the Market-Based Approach to Basic Services

Social policies are needed to ensure equal redistribution of the products of economic growth and welfare. Social policies include several aspects, including access to basic services. These are related to social justice and access of the poor to education and health care.

The *market* neglects the principle of social justice. As stated in the UN's Declaration on the Right to Development, "The right to development … is an inalienable human right by virtue of which every human person and all peoples are entitled to participate in, contribute to, and enjoy economic, social, cultural and political development, in which all human rights and fundamental freedoms can be fully realized." This includes the full range of indivisible, interdependent, and interrelated rights: civil, cultural, economic, political, and social. It calls for a development framework with sectors that mirror internationally guaranteed rights, thus covering, for example, health care, education, housing, justice administration, personal security, and political participation.[21]

In practice, liberalization (opening to foreign providers) or privatization (opening to national private operators) of essential services means that a market-based approach is applied to public services.

By opening essential services provision to foreign private investors and to national private actors, policy makers created two-speed essential services systems, one for the wealthy minority and one for the poor majority. In many cases, essential services provision by the private sector resulted in increased prices in local markets and made health-care and educational services affordable only to the wealthy.

Furthermore, access to water and energy, for example in many rural areas that do not appear profitable enough to private companies, has been reduced over time. Foreign private companies would indeed invest only in areas where there would be a return on their investment. Rural areas represent, in many countries, pockets of poverty and therefore do not have "solvent clients" who can pay for such services.

Persistent and growing structural domestic regulatory frameworks gaps, including the lack of protection of strategic and essential sectors within the national territories, which result from structural adjustment programs, trade

---

[21] Declaration on the Right to Development, available at http://www.un.org/documents/ga/res/41/a41r128.htm.

liberalization, and State disengagement from public services management, have set a negative trend in the implementation of rights for the poor.

Open Questions on Accessing Basic Services and SDGs

How would the SDGs deal with issues deriving from structural domestic regulatory gaps? How would the SDGs manage the market-based approach chosen by many United Nations member states to provide health care and education services?

Overall Challenges

Clarity must be achieved on the proper means to achieve the SDGs, particularly where funding is concerned. The international declarations have proven to be weak when they are not sustained or followed up by real national commitment and proper redistribution strategies at the national level.

Resources are available in many countries that have high levels of poverty.

The political will to face a fair redistribution of the benefits of globalization, including health-care and public education services, is lacking.

Access to services is indeed the key for weaker segments of society. Environmental protection will follow, as people will have higher incomes and an increased awareness of the common good.

PART II

Economic Crisis in Europe: Selected Topics

Thoughts on the Economic Crisis in Europe: Federalism or Failure?

Has Democracy Still a Meaning in Europe?

Following the collapse of the Soviet Union in the late 1980s, the dominant liberal political philosophy all over Europe resulted in the State's withdrawing from its role of acting as a social catalyst and gave the market a role as social developer and economic redistributor. The State has consequently given up its role of service provider in Europe. The current crisis is the consequence of the political choices that allowed the financial markets to take over the real economy. This trend is the logical consequence of what began in the 1980s.

Lack of State and proactive social policies, the weakening of public services, and individualism have resulted in an atomized society where the motto *Sauve qui peut*— "Everyone for himself"—applies. In sum, societies are the sum of individual interests, without a common project.

These national political choices have affected Europe as a whole.

When the financial crisis started, I wondered why the media mostly focused on the private sector as the one that had to "make a gesture," i.e., give up its money! Finally, I understood that government debt was money that had been borrowed from the private banking system! I must admit that this surprised me.

At the same time, it inspired me. *So, for many years, governments had been borrowing on the financial markets without either consulting or informing their citizens. This explains why markets seem to have the power to decide which government policy is more appropriate, so that they can recuperate their funds,* I thought.

Then I asked myself, *What is the role of democracy under the current circumstances?* My feeling is that in the current context, democracy is on hold, as it is actually the financial markets that are managing Europe in a sort of co-management scheme in partnership with governments. The evidence suggests that there cannot be any national democratic control over government decisions relating to economic and financial policies, particularly when such decisions are interlinked with global and European policy making. Therefore, a higher level of regional integration is needed, as well as a stronger role for the European Central Bank in the economic and financial spheres. Europe has more work to do if it wants to integrate its financial and economic policies.

It is, indeed, disheartening to hear debates about countries that are thinking of going back to their national currencies, establishing controls at European frontiers, and revising the Schengen Agreement. Such debates make me think that Europe, as a national democracy, has reached the limit of its ability to create innovative debates.

Instead of looking at the future, some European politicians want to return to the past in a demagogic and even dangerous way. The issue is not the danger that the free movement of people can create! The danger comes, rather, from an inadequate balance between European public policies and markets, as well as from the lack of innovation and employment creation policies in Europe.

National Choices vis-à-vis European Integration ?

Can countries move toward a better future alone? The answer is no! Has any country alone found a solution to the crisis? The answer is, again, no! That is why, finally, the crisis has brought to the top of the agenda the issue of European federalism and integration—and that is, at least, one positive effect of the crisis. European politicians have frequently agreed to find common solutions to the short-term and long-term crises. Surely, this situation is not over. While steps are being taken toward a long-term solution, for many years we have seen the same narrow nationalistic approach and the pursuit of national political interests impede European political integration.

This particularly concerns taxation and foreign policies.

We are all aware that the issue of national sovereignty has always been the main obstacle to the progress of European integration. The Greek crisis has shown that individual State failure affects regional European success and therefore points toward a collective response. But the Italian example is also interesting, as, for many months, the Italian prime minister's credibility had been weakened by a series of incidents which had no concrete impact on national democratic games.

A crisis was reached, and, more specifically, the markets decided that enough was enough. Mr. Berlusconi was replaced. In forty-eight hours, a substantial change took place: first, a government of technicians replaced the so-called democratic government, and a number of new measures were taken in a very short period of time. The question of how citizens choose their politicians in Europe remains open. I always thought that the "personality" of Berlusconi reflected the values—or lack thereof—that underpin Italian society. We are talking about competition based on whom one knows rather than on merit—making easy money through a personal network and connections. Berlusconi's was, indeed, the prototype of a society that lives via the media and refuses to examine its values and societal rules. He was reelected several times despite his inconsistency, both political and personal.

In fact, the values that Berlusconi transmitted fascinated a number of people—particularly men—and related to the super powerful man who commands not because of his ideas and his achievements, but simply because he has money and a dominating attitude. However, the markets no longer trusted him. Even so, had elections taken place in 2011 Berlusconi would have won!

The Italian example raises the question of the accountability of national decision makers in the contemporary European setting. People are worried about their daily lives to the extent that they do not have time to think about the rest of the world. European public opinion is more and more short-sighted and media-dependent. For example, the system of national democratic voting has proved to be inefficient in an economically globalized world. National political representation might, as in the case of Italy, be completely out of step with international reality and carry a country toward marginalization and economic disaster. That is the direction in which Italy was going. At this stage, only a federal Europe can tackle all these challenges. The European population should be made aware that the continent is entering a new era and cannot continue functioning as it did in the last century.

The price of refusing to change would be, and has been, too high, resulting in even more massive unemployment and higher social hurdles.

Thanks to the present economic crisis, Europe can start dealing with serious issues that it has neglected for more than thirty years. Political accountability and the adequacy of economic structures to deal with the international situation are being discussed as a result of a potential collapse of the euro and the implosion of the European economic system. The issue is that reforms will go in the direction of liberalism rather than toward increased social protection.

For example, in Italy, the Monti government had decided to tackle the rigidity of the labor market by liberalizing certain sectors (e.g., taxi licenses and those things that fall under Article 18 of the Constitution of the Italian Republic)–– thereby facilitating its dismissal.

Renzi government that is actually at affairs and it is supposed to be a leftist government in Italy has taken up such an idea that Article 18 must be revised to provide more flexibility to the labor market. The question is that to have flexibility there needs to be opportunities. The Italian labor market provides no opportunities not because enterprises cannot dismiss but because there is no economic policy aiming at industrial and services development.

Therefore, it appears to me that there is a sort of push to the bottom where social development is concerned. The present measures send the message that there is only one way to solve the crisis: to disengage the State even more and to provide more maneuverability for the private sector so that it can be more competitive on the international markets.

The liberal philosophy has advanced even further to solve a crisis that resulted from liberal thinking even within so-called social democratic parties.

It is puzzling.

What about creating the conditions for a more dynamic labor market? What about thinking about measures to reward merit instead of encouraging client networking (this is particularly pertinent for Italy!)? What about having a youth policy that makes possible the creation of innovative businesses without going through heavy administrative procedures?

These questions remain unanswered.

Looking toward the Future or Going Back to the Past?

I am not sure that European societies are moving in the direction of encouraging effort and merit. In fact, my feeling is that such values are disappearing from the social and political spectrum, while the quick-money principle remains fascinating to leaders.

An acknowledged fact is that there is a European brain drain.

Europe has become a region where innovation is seen as subversive and where people are unable to imagine the future––or even create a future. Does this have anything to do with meritocracy? It does. Societies that are stuck in the present cannot imagine the future and therefore do not encourage young people to create and innovate.

Recently, I saw a TV show about Italy. It stated that Italy is not a country made for young people. Italian parents and grandparents provide a home for young people who are unable to move on in life on their own because they cannot find jobs. Actually, unofficially, young people are filling badly paid jobs where one works long hours for a small salary and no social benefits. An amazing situation! In Italy, some people say that when retirees die, the system will collapse, because they are the ones sustaining the Italian economy! And where are the qualified young people? They take on a multitude of small jobs or leave the country.

The Prime Minister Renzi said in a TV program that he sees no problem in brain drain, according to him if valuable Italians can represent Italy abroad it is a honor. That is not the point. The point is that valuable brains should have the choice to stay or leave. The reality is that they leave because intellectual work in Italy is not valued, and it is badly remunerated. The investment made by the educational system is then lost in most cases.

This situation brings me to my next point.

Some European politicians want to reduce immigration flows in Europe and even revise the Schengen Agreement. It is as if Europeans have never migrated or moved around the world. It can only be short-term political interest that compels European politicians to make populist speeches wherein they promote this idea. Speeches like these do not bring any new political ideas to the table. They also give their national constituencies the wrong idea about world politics.

The truth is that if European economies were growing, then Europeans would not fear migration. Someone might say "There is nothing new under the sun." The reality is that European economies are neither creating nor producing new ideas and products. This is a situation that results in a "back to the past" approach. The free movement of people remains a major European achievement. Such an achievement is not questioned. Therefore, it is only demagogy that motivates any questioning. Europeans need concrete solutions to concrete problems, including employment and income generation through innovation and value-added production.

This means initiating a virtual circle and rising to the top instead of continuing to sink to the bottom. It means being guided by hope and confidence rather than by fear of the future and mistrust. This takes more energy and effort, but it is the only way to build a new Europe in the long term.

Turning to the past rather than projecting into and planning for the future will only isolate the continent without solving its structural challenges. Short-term and short-sighted policies resulting from a pragmatic approach have shown their limits. Long-term planning is necessary to formulate appropriate strategies and give hope to European societies.

The increasing inequalities and the "des-integration" of the social structure also have consequences on national security and Europe's relationship with the world. I believe that the social link is the key to fighting against insecurity and extremism of all sorts.

While acknowledging that no system is perfect, I think that there is a certain level of imperfection a system can tolerate before it collapses. We know that the perception of imperfection is different according to the angle from which it is viewed, and also that it depends on a country's stage of economic development and political stability. My reading of the current European system is that it has reached a level of saturation and stagnation, which encourages self-destruction. A sort of social stagnation and fear are embedded into contemporary European societies. There are nuances and differences among countries, but there is a common line of thought: fear of the future!

People fear for the future of their children, fear being less rich in the future, have fear about energy and oil supplies, and so on and so forth.

Europe seems to be stuck in fear while developing few ideas for change and innovation.

Our children will have a future inasmuch as we leave them with values and hope! This is not the case at the moment, as materialism has taken over all the underpinning values that brought us to the present level of economic development: faith in the value of political and social progress!

Europeans are losing hope about something that has inspired the continent for centuries: progress! We are now afraid of losing what we have obtained, and we are neither developing ideas nor creating economic growth.

Fear Is an Obstacle to Innovation

We must learn again that hope inspires entrepreneurship in the sense that it goes beyond making money and reaches the sphere of creation and projection toward a future with an optimistic vision. Of course, international competition is a reality. But what motivates our competitors?

The hope that has motivated the European continent for centuries is that the lives of our descendants will improve as a result of the present generations' development and creation of wealth. It seems that Europeans have lost this motivation. Our comfort has become our prison.

Nevertheless, there is space for hope and improvement, which should encourage optimism.

Europe and Its Youth: What's Happening?

When I Was a University Student ...

As a student in Naples, I faced many challenges, including, among other things, overcrowded university rooms, professors who only remembered me as my registration number (my number was 4,220), and unemployment waiting at the end of my studies.

When the Erasmus program (a European Union–funded program for student mobility in Europe) was publicized at the Istituto Universitario l'Orientale, where I was studying, I thought that my dream of studying abroad for a while could come true. Great!

I passed the exam and won an Erasmus fellowship to complete part of my studies at the University of Louvain-la-Neuve, Belgium. I had no idea what to expect and had never heard of such a university. During my stay in Louvain-la-Neuve, I had a chance to travel from Brussels to Amsterdam, Bruges, and Antwerp by train. I met new friends and learned a new language (Spanish, with a Spanish friend who did not speak French).

The experience changed my life. It opened my eyes to the possibilities offered by a different country. It made me more critical of my own country of origin (Italy) and its dysfunction. It made me a European citizen!

It gave me the chance to gain confidence in myself, as I could adapt to and move around in different countries. I made new friends and discovered the open space of Europe. I felt the hope of "Yes, I can." I became ready to fight for a better place once I returned to my own hometown because I saw that a different reality existed. But most of all, the experience made me a strong supporter of the European project. In fact, without Erasmus, I would have had no chance to study abroad.

Today, I live in Geneva, work in Brussels, and travel for work all over Africa. I feel disheartened by the mistrust I encounter and by the attempt of a few to make us go back to *before* European integration was achieved.

Although I understand those who believe in a national space that protects and guarantees a comfort zone for its citizens, I find something disturbing in that type of reasoning. Do we need to be protected from other human beings because we are unable to continue creating welfare? Do we want to be first to grasp the benefits of the welfare programs already in existence, which we do anyway? What are we afraid of?

When observing the dynamics of the world economy, it is inevitable to note that economic activity is transnational (including illicit economic activities such as mafias). How would a nation alone deal with the complexity of international economic activity as it impacts national employment?

My conclusion is that it is only fear that motivates such a discourse, which simplifies the reality and presents the world as a jungle from which Europeans should withdraw and be protected. Fear also motivated the results of the European elections, which were communicated on May 25, 2014, as well as the results of the vote against the free movement of European people, which took place in Switzerland on February 9, 2014.

While acknowledging the results, I wondered, *What's happening?* After my incredulity subsided came a time for reflection and analysis. My first reaction was this: There is a link between European economic and cultural decadence and the fear of the "unknown" shown in the election results.

In fact, as the services economy develops, the control of European people's movement is very difficult to implement. As a result of the vote of February 9, 2014, the Swiss Confederation has tried hard to fix immigration quotas for Europeans. It is an almost impossible mission.

As a result of these events, a number of thoughts came to my mind. I reviewed the major points I had heard from commentators on the election results and also thought about comments made by my friends.

Poverty Is Spreading All Over Europe

Does the fact that poverty is spreading all over Europe justify the fact that European people wish to "go back to the way things were before"? Before the euro, before free movement, before free trade, before Europe, and before globalization, was reality for Europeans less tough?

The pauperization of the European population is a fact. Poverty is touching middle classes and youth in a dramatic manner all over Europe (with an exception made for

Germany). Youth unemployment is reaching incredibly high points. For instance, in Italy, the average of youth unemployment is 25 percent (which is the national average; in the southern part of the country, it is as high as 46 percent, as revealed in Istat [the Italian National Institute for Statistics] data communicated on June 3, 2014).

The middle class which had been driving European development, is now more and more pauperized. Thus, it has lost its pivotal role in social stabilization. The European elites' optimism, mostly characterized by a faith in a federal Europe, does not account for the growing frustration of the working classes and average citizens who face the challenge of making a living without hope for the future of the European project.

Although they are not aware of the technicalities of the European project and experience difficulty in making a causal link between Europe and the solution of national crises, European citizens are subject to a lack of appropriate industrial and social policies.

Also, they see their incomes eroded by the high cost of living and cannot imagine their children's future because of high unemployment rates, lack of competitiveness, and lack of creativity among European entrepreneurs.

As it goes with public hysteria, an "enemy" has to be found somewhere: the closest one after immigrants is Europe! So, while free-market political philosophy has not brought the welfare expected in Europe, socialist parties have lost their ideological basis.

They have given up on redistributive political aims and have turned toward social-liberal political philosophies.

This centrist shift of socialist parties encouraged extremes to emerge and mobilize Europeans (naturally, with some nuances, depending on countries' national realities. France is more on the right side of the political spectrum, while Spain is more on the left side). All parties claim to pursue the same objective.

Change This Europe! The Question Is, How?

Social dialogue between the capitalists and the working classes to boost growth and make a common project is a challenge, of course. The whole relationship between capital and work must be revised, along with the political thinking of European leaders. They should stop using Europe for their internal electoral purposes, which keeps a more substantial European integration in limbo. This is particularly true as it regards the shift from national to European competence in immigration policies, foreign affairs, defense, and economic and financial management, including employment. National politicians want to convince their electors that they can still impact economic trends, e.g., reduce unemployment.

In reality, in the global economy, national governments do have a smaller and smaller impact on such things. The time has come to admit this fact. It is time to acknowledge that further integration is the only solution. No European nation can face alone international competition—not even France!

Meanwhile, Europe must bring positive results, namely growth and employment. Social dumping in Europe is the result of a lack of serious economic policies at the European level. National states remain ambiguous in this regard. In Italy, for example, the European elections confirmed the Democratic Party as the party in power (it received 40 percent of the vote). Matteo Renzi, the Italian prime minister, has used this result to reinforce his national statement on national reforms without clearly explaining his party's project or his plans for the European project.

Italy Took Over the European Presidency as of July 1, 2014.

Is there a European project proposed by Italy, by the way?

Apparently, Italy will "help to change Europe." It would be useful for Italian citizens to know what the plans are! Italian Prime Minister Matteo Renzi intends to boost demand-driven growth, competitiveness, and employment. These are definitely key issues. As a matter of fact, competitiveness is related to educational and production systems.

The questions that remain open are as follows: How to promote innovation in Europe in general and in Italy in particular? How again to give Europeans confidence in the future?

Matteo Renzi should take appropriate measures, including employment creation measures such as public works and identification of sectors with high employment potential, such as tourism (a totally abandoned and unprofessional sector at the moment); training possibilities abroad for youth and university students; and reestablishing contact with Italians abroad to use their competencies and networks to support the government's action. At the moment, Italians are seen abroad as "privileged" instead of as exported human capital.

Deficit Rules

Deficit rules established by the European Commission caused the current situation. Is there a causality link between the European austerity rule of the 3 percent deficit and the actual stagnation of European economies?

It is because states have overspent and have not promoted or sustained innovation that Europe is in such a deep economic crisis. European institutions do not carry the responsibility for the current situation. Going back to the Europe of nations as well as to national currencies is not the solution, as production models have moved beyond nations.

Furthermore, this crisis results from the nationalist and fragmented approach of European nations in crucial areas such as employment and social policy. National politicians use the European process in their own national interest and shape their discourses on Europe depending on their own national political spectrum: Europe is the cause of national weaknesses when nations do not manage to follow through on electoral promises and when their incompetence to face challenges is shown, as in the case of immigration policies.

It came to my mind that Europe has to move toward deeper and faster integration by shifting from a midway approach (divided between national and European competence) to a more clearly democratically based European system of functioning.

If Europe were able to produce, export, and create welfare rather than poverty, then the immigration issue would be a nonissue, as the economy would be able to absorb both nationals and foreign workers. It is because Europe is lacking in growth, innovation, and welfare that the fear of the "other" is developing.

This fear is encouraged, particularly by the extreme right-wing parties.

Immigration

In reality, in most cases, the immigration percentage remains low as compared to the total European population. Usually, immigrants are employed in jobs at the lowest level of the pyramid and for which no European worker has been available for a while.

However, this trend is changing in some countries, e.g., Italy, where Italians are coming back to jobs previously only performed by Eastern Europeans—for example, elders' care.

In reality, immigration is the other side of the coin of the economic global structure. As it concerns non-European countries' immigration, the relationship between immigration flows and development policies should be reassessed. Historical reasons, e.g., in the case of France and England, and geographical proximity, e.g., in the case of Italy and Spain, are the reasons for regular flows.

Either the dream of a better life or the wish to see "how it is someplace else" is the main motivation for immigration. The international division of labor is still a cause for the hopelessness of the youth population in developing countries. How can that change? It can change if local populations develop an awareness that a better future can only come if people fight for their rights and open up to the world, thereby leaving behind ancient habits and mental dependence on European colonial powers.

The movement of European people is a natural integration-process result that should not be discussed. It sounds like a surreal issue.

What's Next?

By having a right-wing-based European parliament, the European project will turn toward further liberalism and the weakening of European institutions, while bringing more competition among European nations. This is not what it is needed to face international competition and globalization (which will move on, whether Europeans like or not).

We indeed need a stronger Europe and a more integrated federal structure to face the world market and to create a *more socialist Europe.*

The European project opens enormous opportunities for youth and European citizens. It needs, however, clarification and transparency of at least four main issues, namely the following:

1. A deeper political integration process is needed. European leaders should now pass to the next stage, which is federal Europe. Traditional national competencies, namely immigration, defense, and foreign policies, should shift

into the European sphere. European institutions should be strengthened and quality of staff guaranteed through technical competence rather than general intelligence tests. A clear commitment to the European cause should be part of staff recruitment requirements.

2. A campaign focused on the achievements and contribution of European funds and initiatives should be launched in all member states. European initiatives and work are not well-known enough to the general public.

3. An informational campaign to make technical issues such as the budget deficit plain would help decrease the populist space of right-wing parties.

4. The social and demand-driven economic project should be pursued. Italian Prime Minister Matteo Renzi has proposed a more demand-driven Europe. This is a very timely idea. The question is how to strengthen the employment-creation policies? In fact, creation of employment opportunities should be linked to innovation and new sectors' development. Europe remains locked into a traditional-economy view.

5. It distrusts innovative ideas and does not encourage entrepreneurship. A European program should be launched to support and promote new ideas to be developed into businesses.

6. The national educational systems should be revised. In most cases, they remain focused on encyclopedia knowledge, thus discouraging children from creating and "thinking outside the box."

I am a European, I believe in the future, and I want an open and justice-based Europe. It is possible. We should all work toward a more integrated and friendly Europe. Europe has come a long way since 1957. Its efforts shall continue to make Europe an actor of international relevance.

Educational Systems: Impact on Creativity and Economic Innovation (or Lack Thereof) in Europe

In my article "Thoughts on the European Crisis: Federalism or Failure?",[22] I already raised this issue:

> A sort of social stagnation and fear are embedded in the European contemporary societies. Of course, with some nuances and differences among countries but with a common line of thought: fear for the future! Fear for the future of our children, fear of being less rich in the future, fear for energy and oil supplies and so on and so forth.

I made this observation after analyzing the situation of democracy amid the financial crisis in Europe. Lack of innovation and entrepreneurship in Europe is linked to primary and secondary school teaching which does not encourage creativity in Europe.

The following thoughts are inspired by my observation of school dynamics and my exchanges with parents and professionals over the last few years. In light of my exchanges and discussions with parents and professionals, a number of thoughts came to my mind.

---

[22] The full text is available at www.divainternational.ch/spip.php?article716.

In fact, the challenge of seeing children grow-up and being anxious about their performance in school characterizes modern parenting throughout the schooling process.

The following questions are to be asked:

(i)   Why is primary and secondary schooling important for innovation and creativity in Europe?

The link derives from the fact that every adult's "brain model" is forged during the primary and secondary schooling process. Such modeling starts in the primary-school years and continues throughout high school and university. Of course, it is accompanied by extracurricular experiences, including parents' experiences and educational models. However, schooling remains a central part of curriculum construction in the child, who will become an adult.

School performance (earning good marks) remains a central aspect of the present primary and secondary schooling process. While acknowledging that performance is necessary in that it gives one a sense of a child's making an effort to learn, memorize, and absorb knowledge, I see that the issue of inspiring creation and innovation remains open, just as the primary school remains, in my view, a central pillar of an adult's construction.

(ii) Why do major discoveries and technical analyses come mostly from the United States?

The answer is that *inspiration* is a major factor in the United States' educational system, as opposed to control, detention, and fear-based systems (I have mostly the French system in mind).

The US system[23] is experience-based and open to conquer the markets (I am not discussing here the philosophy of the free-market-based economy); the European system remains theoretical and inward-looking. The Europeans' main objective is to create national elites who, in many cases, are not operational outside their national borders and not immediately operational in the national markets.

Particularly in sciences but also in mathematics, the US approach is experience-based, which helps youth to see what happens in reality before they are provided with abstract theory. Also, by encouraging a child to have an independent and autonomous character, the US system provides the tools to forge the spirit of entrepreneurship, which only develops with a willingness to take risks.

In the European approach, theory comes first eventually, experimentation follows (when and if it comes). In this approach, there is no direct path to creation and innovation, as, in many cases, theory does not speak to children who only memorize without really visualizing their scientific learning. In the European system, a child has to conform to a societal scheme aimed at forging a sort of speculative, rather than a creative, mind-set. "Reduce risk to the maximum" is the motto of many European countries.

Risk taking is indispensable to innovation! No risk taking, no innovation!

---

[23] I am aware of the weaknesses and challenges of the primary and secondary schooling systems in the United States.

(iii)   Why, in Europe, are we not managing to forge positive competitive[24] spirits?

First, the learning process is based on a pedagogy of fear (i.e., fear of the teacher, fear of being in retention, and fear of not achieving the average) rather than on a motivation to succeed.

Second, by focusing only on marks and standardized programs, we encourage children to learn information by heart without their even understanding the sense of the learning process. This habit starts early in the primary years and is continued in secondary schools. Children are not in competition to create but in competition for good marks! In some cases, such competition for marks is not motivating enough for the so-called atypical kids, who then lose interest in learning.

After observing a number of schooling experiences and talking with teens, my first answer to the above question is that creativity comes from the encouragement to innovate.

Therefore, a space must be given for children to learn (performance-related) and create (innovation-related) simultaneously. This can only happen if the learning process is linked to the reality of life, not only to the continent's past or a picture in a book!

This means that while students are learning the official standard program, teachers should give them a space to innovate and to question acquired knowledge (this is not to

---

[24] *Positive* here means "aimed at creating, not at undermining and destroying, what exists."

be confused with insolence) by connecting such knowledge to the reality of life and to the future employment market.

Questioning existing knowledge as well as exploring new possibilities must be allowed if kids are to experiment and eventually create. Creativity here is not only intended to mean an artistic activity; it is meant as a potential market innovation. A new formula or a new creation could later become a new market opportunity.

In fact, it is only by testing new approaches that innovation can develop. If the wish to test is inhibited in the child's mind, then creativity will be blocked in the future adult's mind.

In the spirit of the European educational system, the selection process does not aim at selecting the best idea, but rather at preparing a national elite to govern, while excluding, in many cases, the larger number of children (this is particularly true of the French system).

This pedagogical approach is to be questioned, as it impacts adults' critical-thinking and learning processes. A pedagogy based on marks alone puts inevitable emphasis on what needs to be achieved during the year. It does not take into account the potential for innovation and new approaches that can eventually develop among students.

The *box* into which kids have to fit is not elastic. Kids must conform so that the teacher can smoothly go ahead with his or her program. What happens when a student's thinking is outside the box?

That kid either has to conform or leave the school and go somewhere else … If all kids grow up conforming throughout, without even getting the sense of what they learn, how can they develop creativity and innovation?

While acknowledging the need for a standardized program, I do question current pedagogy. Indeed, the students who are *outside the box* (here, I am not referring to pathologies but, rather, to kids who might have a different or a more mature way of thinking as compared to others their age) are not appropriately responded to by the educational system. The system spends much more energy trying to make students fit into the box rather than trying to find appropriate and adapted answers to their specific needs.

The capital of innovation that some students might possess is ignored and wasted. They are to become the *atypical,* if not the *problematic,* profiles, as the standardized system will not be able, in most cases, to integrate them. If fear is used as a pedagogical tool, the result is that children will only learn to pass the year by earning the necessary marks to do so, without really being motivated to understand and create for their own future. The *Internet generation* needs knowledge to be *connected* to reality. Europe has a high youth unemployment rate. It is time to start asking the right questions about the roots of this phenomenon.

European schooling faces a major challenge: providing European youth with the necessary motivation and inspiration to create and innovate for their own futures.

The Trainer Trainee Relationship and Trainees' Attention throughout the Training Sessions

This article intends to share my reflections on the challenges related to adult training. My objective is to provide a perspective on training that results from the equalitarian relationship between the trainer and his or her trainees. The assumption is that an equalitarian relationship between the trainer and the trainee is crucial to setting a trustful training environment.

The equalitarian relationship between the trainer and the trainee is a step toward a participative methodology. The only one that, in my view, is appropriate for adult training. The training context is, therefore, the first step to constructive and results-oriented training. I am assuming that the trainer is prepared and knowledgeable in his or her subject area (the other option is not analyzed here). There are a number of factors that relate to the context in which training takes place. Such factors impact positively or negatively on the training's practical undertaking. Below are ideas that are, in my view, key factors to keeping trainees involved in training.

The Equalitarian Relationship between the Trainer and the Trainees

The trainer's and trainees' equalitarian relationship is shaped as soon as the trainer and trainees enter the training room.

Adult trainees are usually experienced professionals who, in many cases, have decided either to reorient their careers or specialize through training. In both cases, the adult trainee has experience to share and might hold a position of high responsibility outside the training room.

The trainer must be aware of such a reality and, therefore, must avoid infantilizing trainees by underestimating their capacity to be responsible for both their time management and their learning process during the training. The trainee can freely choose his or her level of engagement in the training. Such engagement will depend on the motivation that the trainer is able to instill into the group dynamic, rather than on a hierarchical relationship that the trainer might be tempted to create with the trainees. Instilling trust in the training process is fundamental for a constructive relationship between the trainer and the trainees.

The trainer–trainee relationship must remain an adult relationship between responsible persons. A hierarchical system would guarantee failure. The trainee may play "the child role" while not seriously believing that such a dynamic exists. Such a role would jeopardize learning and the trainees' true engagement in the process. Furthermore, the group would have a tendency to antagonize the trainer. It would be difficult for the trainer to deliver his or her message in this case.

There is a mirror relationship between the trainer and the group. Although the trainer might have a role in sharing knowledge, he or she is not there to show how much he or she knows, but rather to provide trainees with the necessary skills to perform in a given area. Therefore, the trainer should abstain from diverging from the subject matter. Focus is a must.

Trainees' Attention throughout the Training

The level of attention of trainees will depend on the relationship that the trainer creates with the group in the first minutes of contact. Making eye contact and shaking hands are the first trust-setting acts. The trainer will have to put him- or herself in the shoes of the trainees to understand what types of difficulties they might encounter in their daily working lives and how such a context affects their learning process. Refusing to make this type of contextual analysis would jeopardize the trainer's chances to be "taken onboard" by the group.

The trainer needs the group's empathy if he or she is to be trusted and listened to. To keep trainees' level of attention focused throughout the training, the trainer has to be mindful of trainees' facial expressions and frequently ask them questions related to the content and/or ask them to provide inputs to support the content of the presentation (I refer here to substance training, where content is highly technical, rather than to open-ended training). Asking questions usually allows participants to assess the level of their technical knowledge, thus allowing the trainer to adapt his or her presentation to the level of participants' knowledge (see previous section). The group senses when the trainer is not genuine and is trying to bluff during question-and-answer sessions. In practice, this means that if the trainer does not know the reply to a question, then it is better for him or her to tell the group that the reply will be provided at a later stage, after the trainer consults the appropriate documents. This is a different case from one in which the trainer does not fully understand the question. Here, the trainer might ask the inquisitor whether he or she properly understood the question posed.

Participation of trainees should be encouraged. Some trainers have a tendency to put trainees in a situation where they are hesitant to ask questions, for fear of not being able to reply. This is a wrong methodology, as it shuts down communication, which is a key factor in a participatory training context.

Delivering the messages of the training after taking into account the group's level of knowledge is another key factor in successful training. Trainers should focus on continuously assessing (not evaluating!) the participants' level of knowledge by asking questions related to the topic in order to keep trainees' attention focused on the training content (an adult's attention span is quite short).

This technique will help the trainer to adapt messages so that they speak to the group's knowledge base. There is no point in going into details when participants have already mastered the subject or when they have not yet mastered the general concepts.

In both cases, the risk is "losing them" in the process. The practice of drawing attention to complex sides of the issue at stake, rather than trying to clarify concepts, can frustrate trainees, thereby discouraging them from listening and staying motivated.

There is no point, either, in going too fast—this is a risk particularly when one uses slides—if the group is composed of beginners who will not retain details, as they will have to first memorize basic concepts.

A one-size-fits-all approach to training does not respond to the group's needs and will frustrate trainees. Training is definitely a demand-driven activity. Trainers should abstain from imposing their needs on the participants. Rather, they should be mindful of the group's level of knowledge and practical needs.

There are cases where the group is heterogeneous. When the group is characterized by different levels of knowledge and experience, the trainer should maintain a good balance between the beginners and the "experts" of the group. In practice, this means avoiding focusing too much on the "strongest" participants. First, the risk is that the trainer can make mistakes if the perspectives and experiences of the "experts" are wrong (for example, in cases where experiences do not comply with legal texts). Second, the trainer might lose the control of the group dynamic, as other trainees will sense that the trainer is somehow carried away by only a few people.

The group dynamic will be disrupted and the trainer's credibility diminished. More-experienced participants can share their experiences with the group, which is always enriching, but the trainer must remain in control of the group dynamic and the training objectives—and avoid being carried away.

Conclusions

Adult training is a challenging activity. The trainer has a crucial role to play in making the training useful and successful.

The trainer has to be aware of any knowledge challenges faced by trainees. If the trainer is on a cloud and out of touch with the trainees' realities, then his or her performance will be mismatched to the trainees' needs and expectations.

I have shared some ideas on training context based on experience. These are not meant to be exhaustive but, rather, to provide some hints for those who are engaged in training as a tool for social development.

Equality between the trainee and the trainer is a key factor in the success of an effort to provide information to experienced adults. The trainer and the adult trainees are on equal footing, although the trainer is providing a specific supplement to the trainees' experience.

Global Conclusions

The fight against poverty is to be pursued worldwide.

This fight requires more representative multilateral institutional functioning and innovative national policies.

The thoughts in this book show the red line that exists between the multilateral stall and a number of political and economic principles of liberal philosophy. Such principles, pushed to the extreme, have negatively impacted the financial economy and the real economy alike, as greed has taken over the idea of the balance of power and of control over economic activity.

In "Thoughts on the European Crisis: Federalism or Failure?"

I already raised the following issue of fear as a blockage factor for innovation and development in Europe. The economic standstill in Europe is not only linked to the international market crisis but also to lack of creativity and spirit of enterprise in its large sense. This situation is the result of encyclopedia knowledge. This reflection led me to analyze the interface between the economic crisis and the way in which democracies are facing the challenges posed by the globalized world. I hope that this book has provided you with an innovative interpretation of the current world and its challenges.

Sources

Reports

1944 Declaration of Philadelphia, Constitution of the International Labour Office.

Institute of Social Studies – Netherlands – Strategies of Innovation snd Training for Senior Administrators in Africa, Jean-Martin Tchaptchet, 1976.

Alamgir, M., and P. Agor. *Providing Food Security for All,* IFAD Studies in Rural Poverty 1 (New York: New York University Press, 1991).

Assemblée Parlementaire du Conseil de l'Europe, Session Régulière, Strasbourg, 2002.

Assemblée Nationale de France, L'Organisation Mondiale du Commerce: Une Entreprise Inachevée, Documents d'Information, report no. 2,948.

Communication from Benin on behalf of the African group, World Trade Organization document WT/AFT/W/21, June 2006.

Communication from Zambia on behalf of the LDC group, World Trade Organization document WT/AFT/W/22, June 2006.

ILEAP, "The Financial Architecture of Aid for Trade, Executive Summary," Background Brief 9, April 2006.

International Labour Office, Conseil d'Administration, GB276/WP/SDL, 276th session, Geneva, November 1999.

———, "Des valeurs à défendre, des changements à entreprendre la justice sociale dans une économie qui se mondialise: un projet pour l'OIT." Report of Director-General, 81st session, Geneva, 1994.

———, "Le travail dans le monde 1997/98 Relations professionnelles, démocratie et cohésion sociale," Geneva, November 4, 1997.

Recommendations by the Task Force on Aid for Trade, World Trade Organization document WT/AFT/1.

"Summary of Contributions from Intergovernmental Organizations: Aid for Trade Task Force," World Trade Organization document WT/AFT/W/17, June 2006.

Report by the Committee on Agriculture to the General Council, World Trade Organization document G/AG/16/, June 1, 2006.

World Bank, "Global Economic Prospects for Developing Countries" (Washington, 1993).

———, "Indicateurs du développement dans le monde," 2001.

———, "Workers in an Integrating World," World Development Report (New York: Oxford University Press, 1995).

———, World Development Report (Washington, 1987).

Report on a conference organized by UNCTAD and the Commonwealth Secretariat, United Nations, New York and Geneva, 2006.

UNCTAD Report on LDCs, September 2006.

United Nations Development Programme, "Making Global Trade Work for People" (London: Earthscan Publications, Ltd., 2003).

Books and Reviews

Aglietta, M., *Régulation et Crises du Capitalisme,* ed. Odile Jacob (Paris: Opus, 1997).

Allemand, S., and J. C. Ruano-Borbalan, *La Mondialisation: Le Triomphe du Libéralisme Sauvage* (Paris: Editions de l'Hèbe, 2002).

Bourdieu, P., *Contre-Feux, Raisons d'Agir* (Paris: Seuil, 1998).

―――. *Contre-Feux 2, Raisons d'Agir* (Paris: Seuil, 2001).

Bourguinat, H., *Internationalisation et Autonomie de Décision* (Paris: Economica, 1982).

Polanyi, K., "Societies and Economic Systems" in *The Great Transformation: The Political and Economic Origins of Our Time* (Boston: Beacon Press, 1944), 43–55.

Gilpin, R., *US Power and the Multinational Corporation— The Political Economy of Foreign Direct Investment* (New York: Basic Books, Inc., Publishers, 1975).

Gosta-Esping, A., "The Three Political Economies of the Welfare State" in *Power Resources Theory and the Welfare State: A Critical Approach,* ed. Julia S. O'Connor and Gregg M. Olsen (Toronto: University of Toronto Press, 1998).

Gramsci, A., *Selections from the Prison Notebooks of Antonio Gramsci* (New York: International Publishers, 1971).

Rodrick, Dani, "The Global Governance of Trade as if Development Really Mattered" (paper presented for the Trade and Sustainable Human Development Project) (New York: United Nations Development Programme, 2001).

www.ingramcontent.com/pod-product-compliance
Lightning Source LLC
Chambersburg PA
CBHW050407290526
45786CB00003B/1158